Full Breath of Gratitude

A journal for reclaiming your passion and purpose

By Chris Craig MSW, MPCC

Printed by Chris Craig, through Bookbaby
Printed in the United States of America.
Available from Amazon.com, Walmart.com, Barnsandnoble.com other retail outlets

Written & Designed by Chris Craig, MSW, MPCC

Contributing editor, Chris Kozlouski

Cover art by Susan Craig, 734-475-7886, Facebook Sue Craig – Michigan Impressionist

Art Therapist, Art Opportunities, Chris Kozlouski

Disclaimer

Continue the conversation

Facebook group: Full Breath of Gratitude, to share stories and participate in discussions around gratitude and abundant living.

To book speaking, workshop or consulting services for individual, Church, business or nonprofit please contact: Chris Craig Stolenhoursconsulting@gmail.com 70P-urp-ose9, (707-877-6739)

Dedication

The Full Breath of Gratitude is dedicated to my parents Rod and Sue Craig. Their emotional, spiritual, and loving support has been a lifelong guide for a life well-lived. My dad passed away from cancer in March 2021; my prayer is that this book will honor his passion for justice and equality for all people. My parents are beloved by their community, church, and family. I believe it was their passion for living their lives in a spirit of gratitude and abundance which has been the root of my work and this book.

Author

Chris Craig received his Masters in Social Work from Tulane University and his Masters in Pastoral Care & Counseling at Garrett Seminary. Over his career, Chris has worked as a Director of Correctional Ministries, run family shelter programs, has done consulting with churches and businesses, and provided decedent care as a chaplain for hospitals. Chris has a passion for progressive interfaith spiritual formation that builds a people's sense of purpose from the inside out.

His Stolen Hours consulting business develops inspirational journals and books that motivate people to live their passions and purpose—creating motivational material that pulls people's minds and spirits from personal success goals to how they might establish a life with significance. Chris seeks to be a speaker, writer, and thought leader using journals, videos, and books that prompt people to live their life's calling mindfully and playfully out loud.

In Chris's new book, **Full Breath of Gratitude,** Chris has developed a journal for reclaiming one's passion and purpose through an internal daily practice of gratitude. Making space for gratitude is by no means a quick-fix, self-help, fly-by-night tool. As readers contemplate gratitude, they will need to consider what obstructions are keeping them from making changes in their lives. Obstruction comes from the Latin' *obstruere,* which means to block up from a movement of air.

The first part of the book looks at nine obstacles to a life based in gratitude. Many of us are hard-wired to resist the possibility of change. Even when the books offer prescriptions which are as simple as self-discipline or straightforward suggestions of a different way to look at life, we rebel at the idea of change even when the suggestions are well within our capabilities. When we consider some of the inner paradigm shifts that could occur, suddenly, there are often obstacles or obstructions that could come up when you consider a new breath in your gratitude.

The second part of the book is a 30-day gratitude journal that offers tools and prompts to assist people with an internal exploration into a new life perspective of abundance. The Full Breath of Gratitude explores nine obstructions that people encounter when considering a life based on gratitude.

Contributing Editor & Art Opportunities

Chris Kozlowski is a practicing Art Therapist with many years of experience working with both children and adults. She has worked in various settings including inpatient mental health, residential treatment for adolescents, and a shelter for children waiting for foster placement. She received her Masters of Art in Art Therapy from the Art Institute of Chicago. She currently works at the School of Expressive Arts and Learning (in Lombard, IL) and helps children with special needs find their creative voices through the art process. In addition, Chris also received her Masters of Divinity degree from Garrett Seminary (in Evanston, IL.) She has performed many weddings of all kinds, and has recently been appointed as the Director of Children's Ministry at the First United Methodist Church in Lombard, IL. She currently lives with her wife and two young children just outside of Chicago. She believes her calling in life is to "help others to find their voices through the creative process"

CONTENTS

Full Breath of Gratitude

How to read this book

"As we express our gratitude, we must never forget that the highest appreciation is not to utter words, but to live by them."

— *John F. Kennedy*

T he power of a journal is that it is not linear; you begin

and stop where you need to. Rather than being a book with a clear beginning, middle and end, this piece is meant to be a reflective journal made up of distinct expressions that encompass a full breath of gratitude. It is actually part book and part journal... the book part has themes and ideas which might challenge your perceptions. The journal piece has questions and exercises which are meant to capture and hone in on the "light of gratitude" and aspects of your story in new and more profound ways. Just as a full breath involves drawing in air and releasing it again, so too are the two different parts of this book intended to function as one cohesive whole, balancing each other out.

Many of you have already read books or done meditations on gratitude. Thus, whether you are a newcomer or a regular to this type of reflection, there may be a myriad of reasons why you have found this book. I have written this reflective journal so that each chapter, exercise, and workbook piece is able to stand alone. The book and your own personal experience will guide the way you use it according to your individual needs.

You may find yourself returning to the book at different times for different reasons. Perhaps one day you might be in search of journaling starters for reflection, and another time you may pick it up for new takes, insights, or perspectives around inner knots which might be binding you from a life of gratitude. On one day you might read an "Obstructions to Gratitude" piece and then tackle a reflective journaling workbook piece to sharpen your mind. Another day you might just need to capture your previous day's moments of gratitude with the "Five & One tool." Yet another time, you might just feel a need for creative expression and seek to express appreciation or explore ideas in a more visual, artistic, or tangible way by utilizing one of the Art Opportunities found at the end of a chapter.

The English novelist E.M. Foster once reflected on his piece <u>Longest Journey,</u> *"I suggest that the only books that influence us are those for which we are ready, and which have gone a little further down our particular path than we have yet gone ourselves."*

Whether you need to inhale a new perspective, exhale your own experience or simply hold your breath for a moment and have a space to "just be..." you should feel free to browse the table of contents, or just stick your finger in the book randomly and begin to explore at any point you like. This book could be a one-time read from cover to cover, or you could keep it close on your shelf as a resource that you open up for inspiration as you need it. You may even find yourself using it as a lifetime tool where you read the same pieces or explore the same questions every couple of years to discover how your perspective and or story has grown and shifted. Treat this book as a personal reflective piece where you can catch your current breath of gratitude at whatever point you currently reside.

Introduction

I don't know about you, but it seems like the world we live in always seems to be focused on "more." If I just had _____, I would not be angry. If I had this car, house, relationship, or job, I could be happy. The idea is that the world would tell you when you're "enough..." or that an alarm would go off in your head when you had enough status, faith, money, power, love, homes, jobs, freedom, etc. Many of us have inner voices that tell us that if we could just reach _____, we would not feel angry, empty, depressed, or so very alone.

But how much stuff is enough? How high would you have to reach to have others deem you to be successful? Or before you could allow yourself to "feel" successful? Most of us want our lives, our work, our relationships to be experienced as significant; we want our lives to matter. But at the end of the day, what have we done with what we already have? Have we utilized our gifts? Have we treasured the relationships we have or the people we encounter throughout our lives?

What have we done with the money, power, knowledge, and opportunities with which life has already blessed us?

Often in our search for more, we get caught in a mental loop of feeling like we are never good enough. When we consider how entrenched we are in our need for more and how much we define our worth around the things we feel we do not have, then we begin to understand the value of gratitude.

Think about this: we are born naked, and then our parents feed us, clothe us and introduce us to the communities we grow up in. Our communities quickly begin to tell us what we need to do in order to be accepted if we want to be seen as being successful. So, in a sense, "needing more" is not native to us. We are born into a world that naturally feeds and nourishes us, but it is the world outside ourselves that tells us we must constantly want more and "be more" in order to be deemed significant.

Appreciation for what one has challenges our notion of a world of scarcity... the idea that there is not enough in the world and especially that there is not enough for YOU. All of a sudden something shifts in a person's mind when each day they transition their thoughts from considering what they need to what they have been blessed with and currently have.

This journal is meant to be a launching platform-- a thirty-day tool to slowly and quietly dismantle your habit of running towards getting more "things." The exercises begin a mental and spiritual journey toward abundance, which could awaken you to a new sense of fullness of your life and the world around you.

THE BEGINNING

The 100 Question Journey

"In Search Of"

Gratitude

In the face of loss
Or the shadow of doubt
It's the gentle hope
That will lift you out

It's the tender smile
Or the whispered sigh
It's the lack of an answer
And the wondering why

It's embracing a moment
When you don't know how
It's releasing the past
And digging in to the "now"

It's allowing the future
To settle in to today
It's speaking the words
Or learning to pray

It's holding a breath
And then letting go
It's running the race
And then walking slow

It's opening up
And taking a chance
It's sharing the journey
Or softening your stance

It's extending a hand
And not feeling "above"
It's a humbling feeling
And learning to love

It's admitting when you've
strayed
And understanding what's
right
Stepping out of the darkness
And basking in the light

It's forgiving yourself
And those who've done wrong
It's finding your purpose
And where you belong

It's owning your mistakes
But not letting them define you
It's trusting again
And letting faith find you

It's finding your voice
And speaking out loud
It's the moments that are quiet
And the ones that are proud

It's the littlest thing
That now seems worthwhile
It's knowing we're saved
By inches not miles

It's accepting the things
That aren't exactly your plan
It's living with uncertainty
But believing you can

It's the thank-you we say
Before we're fully awake
It's the thoughtful goodbye
And the next step you take

Gratitude

Poem by Chris Kozlowski

THE BEGINNING

THE 100 QUESTION JOURNEY

T he first place I attempted this transformative exercise

was with a group of homeless families living in a shelter community. A woman in a shelter is surrounded by a world of emptiness, uphill battles in every direction. Finding employment, childcare, often balancing children's and personal regrets regarding money and relationships. Some running from abusive relationships, others from mistakes with landlords, family or debts that simply got away from them.

Needless to say, the mental/spiritual journey from seeing one's life as full of obstacles and scarcity to that of seeing a world of possibilities and abundance is a long road. However, if fear is going to be overcome, steps in the direction of hope need to be taken. Fear causes us to isolate and freeze up; fear causes us to focus on all the things we are not and that we do not have. You do not have to be homeless to understand a need to want to have more or be more in a desire to reach happiness.nin

This is the exercise I used with these homeless families as a jumping off point toward a new outlook, direction, and sense of peace. If you take the time and allow yourself to be vulnerable enough to invest yourself fully into these questions, they can be a transformative first step towards a new, fresh outlook and roadmap into the rest of your life. This exercise worked so well that I started using it with church groups, non-profits and several big and small businesses.

Like so many things in life, the question this exercise asks is so simple... and yet so profound and difficult the deeper you allow yourself to dive into it. There is a famous Chinese religious text called the Tao-Te-Ching which begins with the words, "The beginning of a million-mile journey begins with the first step." This". Well, this exercise is a 100-question journey and could be a first step towards a life of *hope, significance, and abundance.*

> *GRATITUDE:*
>
> *It's finding your voice*
>
> *And speaking out loud*
>
> *It's the moments that are quiet*
>
> *And the ones that are proud*
>
> *By Chris Kozlouski*

On the next page you will find one question written 100 times: "I am so grateful for _____". Just know that what seems like an easy question to answer 3, 5, or 9 times could grow more complex once you reach 17, 30, or 60 times. This series of questions should not be considered a race; you should give yourself plenty of emotional time and space as your mind has to dig and drudge through all the things you are and all things you have never considered being grateful for. I must tell you: for a lot of people there are going to be many moments during this exercise where they want to walk away, as their mind pleads with them to allow it to come back to the questions later. DO NOT STOP. Push; push through all 100 questions, whether your answers are initially surface and shallow, or thoughtful and deep. This book, this journey is offers the possibility of a whole new life perspective. Your million-mile journey begins with this "first step" and 100 questions.

As you begin, please utilize the first "I am so grateful for _____" to share your thanksgiving's for (God, Jesus, Buddha, Mohammed, the Universe, positive energy or) whatever greater power you want to thank, if you desire to do so. Though it is important to share thanks to that which is greater than you or created you, the power in this exercise is more about the abundance which is and has been in your life and less about who or what brought it about.

I have had groups who have taken a half-hour or an hour to dive into this exercise. I have also had small groups who say they have taken an afternoon or evening to dive into the questions. Again, the time, space, whether you are doing it alone, in a small group or in a large one does not matter. What does matter is that you push through all 100 questions.

100 Moments of Gratitude

1. I am so grateful for _____ *(God, Jesus...)*
2. I am so grateful for _____
3. I am so grateful for _____
4. I am so grateful for _____
5. I am so grateful for _____
6. I am so grateful for _____
7. I am so grateful for _____
8. I am so grateful for _____
9. I am so grateful for _____
10. I am so grateful for _____
11. I am so grateful for _____

Those were easy, you still have 89 more

12. I am so grateful for _____
13. I am so grateful for _____
14. I am so grateful for _____
15. I am so grateful for _____
16. I am so grateful for _____
17. I am so grateful for _____
18. I am so grateful for _____

19. I am so grateful for _____

20. I am so grateful for _____

21. I am so grateful for _____

22. I am so grateful for _____

23. I am so grateful for _____

24. I am so grateful for _____

25. I am so grateful for _____

26. I am so grateful for _____

27. I am so grateful for _____

28. I am so grateful for _____

29. I am so grateful for _____

I never thought of being thankful for these things, only 70 more to go

30. I am so grateful for _____

31. I am so grateful for _____

32. I am so grateful for _____

33. I am so grateful for _____

34. I am so grateful for _____

35. I am so grateful for _____

36. I am so grateful for _____

37. I am so grateful for _____

38. I am so grateful for _____

39. I am so grateful for _____

40. I am so grateful for _____

41. I am so grateful for _____

42. I am so grateful for _____

43. I am so grateful for _____

44. I am so grateful for _____

45. I am so grateful for _____

46. I am so grateful for _____

47. I am so grateful for _____

48. I am so grateful for _____

49. I am so grateful for _____

50. I am so grateful for _____

51. I am so grateful for _____

52. I am so grateful for _____

53. I am so grateful for _____

54. I am so grateful for _____

55. I am so grateful for _____

56. I am so grateful for _____

57. I am so grateful for _____

This is often where the tears come only more 43 left

58. I am so grateful for _____

59. I am so grateful for _____

60. I am so grateful for _____

61. I am so grateful for _____

62. I am so grateful for _____

63. I am so grateful for _____

64. I am so grateful for _____

65. I am so grateful for _____

66. I am so grateful for _____

67. I am so grateful for _____

68. I am so grateful for _____

69. I am so grateful for _____

70. I am so grateful for _____

71. I am so grateful for _____

72. I am so grateful for _____

73. I am so grateful for _____

74. I am so grateful for _____

75. I am so grateful for _____

76. I am so grateful for _____

77. I am so grateful for _____

78. I am so grateful for _____

79. I am so grateful for _____

80. I am so grateful for _____

81. I am so grateful for _____

82. I am so grateful for _____

83. I am so grateful for _____

84. I am so grateful for _____

85. I am so grateful for _____

86. I am so grateful for _____

87. I am so grateful for _____

88. I am so grateful for _____

89. I am so grateful for _____

90. I am so grateful for _____

91. I am so grateful for _____

92. I am so grateful for _____

93. I am so grateful for _____

94. I am so grateful for _____

95. I am so grateful for _____

96. I am so grateful for _____

97. I am so grateful for _____

98. I am so grateful for _____

99. I am so grateful for _____

    I am so grateful for _____

You made it!!!!!!!

Let's Talk

At what number did the exercise get difficult? _____

What surprised you about the exercise?

_____

_____

_____

_____

Was there any item that you never thought of being grateful for before this exercise?

_____

_____

_____

Looking back at your list, do you see any themes of things you are especially grateful for?

_____

_____

How did you feel when you finished the exercise? Did you your perspective of the world change at all?

_____

_____

_____

OBSTRUCTIONS

Barriers to gratitude

OBSTRUCTIONS TO GRATITUDE:

There are countless reasons we pick up self-help, how-to books as well as spiritual formation books; they have a strange allure. I think we often pick them up because we think they might speak to some of our inner longings to feel known, connected, and whole. Other times we might pick them up because we are looking for something to show us a quick way to success, a magical formula which might give us power over our pain, anxiety and fear of failure.

However, too often we end up discouraged, first because there is no such thing as a quick fix. And second, because many of us are hard-wired to resist the possibility of change. Even when the books offer prescriptions which are as simple as self-discipline or straightforward suggestions of a different way to look at life, we rebel at the idea of change even when the suggestions are well within our capabilities. There is just something that feels safe about the emptiness or struggle you already know, compared to the unknown. Making space for Gratitude is by no means a quick-fix, self-help, fly-by-night tool. But when you consider some of the time, worldview, and inner paradigm shifts that could occur, suddenly there are several obstacles or obstructions that could come up as you consider a new breath in your gratitude.

Obstruction comes from the Latin *'obstruere* which means to block up from a movement of air. As we contemplate a full breath of gratitude, we need to consider what obstructions often occur which keep us from making changes in our lives. In part II we are going to explore nine obstructions that people encounter when they begin to consider a life based in gratitude.

Nine Obstructions to Gratitude:

1. **We believe our stuff makes us happy**
   Abundance of "SHTUFF", looks at how our worldview is made up of our perspective around how much stuff we think we need to be enough. It looks at how a life of gratitude makes peace with both the worldviews of abundance and scarcity.

2. **We believe in a world of absolutes**
   The piece Absolutes explores how the way we try to define our realities as being black and white, one way or the other, could be keeping us from a lifetime of opportunities. What if

our assumptions were not made into foregone conclusions? What if our assumptions could be reimagined as a "work-in-progress"? When we allow ourselves to experience the question instead of requiring an answer, then we are open to possibilities instead of reacting to life in bursts of ignorance

3. **Afraid there is not enough to go around**
    Choosing your reality, dives into our fears of a world of scarcity. Is the world one full or opportunities or is there a set number of choices and you better do all you can do to get yours before the world runs out. The two most important words that people must understand if they to claim (or reclaim) their lives are ***reality*** and ***choice***. The way we think the world works is what most of us call our ***reality***.

4. **Our inner wounded child**
    Message to your inner child, looks at how many of us in our adolescence had inner story maps that depicted a world of struggle and

scarcity. Childhoods full of stories that told you –life is hard, opportunities are hard to come by. Childhood stories that have not been given space to evolve. How we interpret our place in the world, sets the basis for whether we see a world of abundance.

5. **We are afraid to be still**

   The What if I could be still piece explores how a life of gratitude involves time for stillness and refection. And many of us, are afraid of standing still. What scares us about being still? Do you think if you were in silence that you would be flooded with voices telling you you're "not enough"? Or are you more afraid that the silence would rupture an inner dam of views which, up to now, have been whispering, "You have so much more to offer, why have you been hiding your gifts and talents?"

6. **The great lie**

   The great lie explores the falsehood that today must be like yesterday and tomorrow is going to be like today. The most damaging part of the lie—that today must be like yesterday—is that people's suffering is born out an attempt to hold today as it was yesterday, or as they believe or remember it was. The act of grief is natural; it means you truly loved and are going to miss the person or moment in time. But suffering occurs when we try to maintain a certain moment of time. The great lie wants to hold moments still and live for them as they once were.

7. **Gratitude sounds weak**
In the piece <u>Power</u>, we explore how the act of gratitude can sometimes be experienced internally as an expression of weakness. This obstruction explores how we might redefine being grateful as another choice that involves power. A boss who is riding you at work, or a fellow student who seems to be bullying you can either empower or defeat you. In the light of gratitude, you can choose to see the world from the bully's eyes, ...what is their perspective?

8. **Feel out of control**:
   In <u>Not Enough</u>, we will delve into the struggle of never feeling like we are enough. The feeling that we have not chosen our experience, but instead our reality has chosen us. And we will explore the even deeper question of "how we are supposed to show gratitude in a world filled with struggle, pain and grief? What does suffering have to do with a spirit of gratitude, knowing that we cannot fix things in the end?

9. **Nostalgia**
   <u>Suffering & Healing</u> looks at our natural desire to want to fix –things, people and moments. Fixing is about returning someone or something back to a simpler or perfect state. We need to remember that even if a bone heals when it is bandaged, it is not the same bone; it is a new creation. We want to hold things as they were, or how we believe they were in Suffering and healing.

Breathe in...
You HAVE ENOUGH
Exhale...
"ENOUGH"
Inhale a sense of purpose
Exhale...knowing you HAVE ENOUGH

ABUNDANCE OF "SHTUFF"

1. *We believe our stuff makes us happy*

U sually, when we consider a world of plenty or

scarcity, we are focused on what we believe our level of opportunity is. Questions of wealth swirl around in our heads and surround our perceived ability to achieve the things we think we "have to" achieve. We make a mental list of our needs... the things that we believe will bring us happiness as well as give an outside appearance of success. After all, the Jones's are not going to keep up with themselves! When we think of scarcity and opportunity in the world, we ask questions such as: how much money, how many cars, how big a house or apartment, how much "shtuff" is going to be *enough*. Scarcity is that voice in our heads that tells us that there is only a finite amount of opportunity in the world -- an ever-dwindling amount of projects, jobs, money, and imaginative ideas -- and if I do not hurry, they are all going to run out!

A life of gratitude makes peace with both the worldviews of abundance and scarcity. Gratitude says, "I appreciate what I have and want to live the wealth of opportunities thoroughly before me." At the same time, appreciativeness may also awaken the knowledge that the world is scarce --that you are blessed because you have so much. Gratitude is the reminder of what you have accomplished despite all the injustice and struggle in the world. Gratitude says I am a survivor, not a victim; I honor both the little and much I have.

Art Opportunity:

Draw a picture of what *"being rich"* means to you. Is it about possessions? ...security? ...people? ...love?

Feel free to include as much details and as many people/places/qualities/things that represent *"true wealth"* to you.

Breathe in love...now hold that breath
Exhale change
Breathe in hope...hold it
Exhale tears

Remember neither your fears nor your joys
are absolute. You interpret the meaning of
every feeling and breath

ABSOLUTES

2. *WE BELIEVE IN A WORLD OF ABSOLUTES*

It is said that the Buddha began as a child with the

worshipping of **things**. Born a prince, the Buddha had
lots of "stuff" and people at his beck and call. Yet, to his
wonderment, he still didn't have peace, and he could
not find happiness. The Buddha decided to abandon
his father's castle and retreated to caves and trees to
learn how to deny himself. What he ultimately realized
is that, whether he was chasing **things** or running from
them, any time he thought he found an absolute
answer, it inevitably ended in despair.

I was raised as a Christian with the idea that belief in God needed to be absolute. God-language was absolute language: "I am the way, truth, life!" Yet as I look at the world around me, most of what God has taught me about the world has not been based on a set of absolutes. The resurrection, the Exodus, and parables such as the Prodigal Son are all about shifting, movement, and changes in people's lives and the times they lived in.

Elizabeth Mattis-Namgyal, in her book, "<u>The Power of an Open Question</u>", asks us: *"Can we... ever reach absolute conclusions about the redness of a flower, a moment of grief, or the meaning of the universe?"*

Stop and think for a moment about all of the assumptions and conclusions we make day in and day out. There are the likes or dislikes on Facebook, our opinions during conversations in cafes or bars, the small talk by the water cooler, the gossip as we pass people we know... we are constantly thinking about who we are and how we want to look to others throughout our days. Is there ever such a thing as certainty about any of our questions? Can there ever be a time where we are able to reach a place of absolute certainty about any of our conclusions?

> *"Certainty traps us into seeing our assumptions as forgone conclusions rather than as a 'work-in-progress'. "*

Or is there such a thing as approaching life as an **open-ended question**? By approaching life as an *open-ended question* we are protected from our natural mental extremes. Certainty traps us into seeing our assumptions as foregone conclusions rather than as a "work-in-progress". When we allow ourselves to experience the question instead of requiring an answer, then we are open to possibilities instead of reacting to life in bursts of ignorance.

When you try to experience life as an open-ended question, you are giving yourself permission to address each moment and the problem you encounter with a feeling of opportunity, freedom, and creative intelligence.

I can just hear the bells going off in your head; are you saying that *absolute truths* and standing for something absolutely is wrong? After all, isn't the old saying true that, "If you don't stand for something, then you will fall for anything?" Honestly, I think there is a time for free-thinking.

You might want to think about absolutes in life like a rock or a log that is placed in moving water (life). The stone or log (like our absolutes) naturally erodes over time. The rock or log allows itself to change with fast-moving water or waves.

Thinking about life as an open-ended-question is like experiencing life as a good boxer who can move around his opponents' fists. If the boxer stands too firm then they will unavoidably take the full blows of their opponent. The fighter must bob and weave with the punches and the energy of their challenger.

Living in gratitude makes it possible to stand in front of life without so many judgments. The act of being grateful allows us to explore our lives as an open-ended question. When we are thankful, then we are open to essential questions, open to our feelings, and open to the story of life that is unfolding before us.

Art Opportunity:

Draw something that remains uncertain that you are currently at peace with or are currently working on being peaceful with. It can be something you once desired to be stable or absolute but now see the value in releasing it and accepting it as a work in progress. It can be something you struggled with in the past but now can embrace as ever changing and evolving. Draw as much detail as you feel able.

*With your eyes closed can you recall the
temperature that day, your surroundings or
any words that were said?*

What made this moment meaningful?

CHOOSING YOUR REALITY

3. *AFRAID THERE IS NOT ENOUGH TO GO AROUND*

As you begin to risk seeing a world of plenty and

being open to a world of opportunities instead of a
world of scarcity, your overall worldview will begin to
shift. This shift can alter your whole sense of place in
the world. You will start to understand that one of your
greatest gifts is your power to ascribe personal meaning
to life events. The power to attribute **meaning** is
simply the ability to interpret your circumstances and
stories in ways that move your role in the story of your
life from that of a victimized character to that of an
empowered survivor.

Once a person can ascribe an empowered meaning to an event, then they are given personal license to **reframe** events to allow them to fit into their **best life** and a new grace-driven worldview.

We cannot stop the world from changing; everything of substance has an end if it had a beginning. Suffering is caused by trying to hold things as they were, or as we believe they were. Our memories and our stories should remind us of where we have been or even the possibilities of where we might be able to go. But memory should never be trusted or worshiped above the potential of our current reality.

The two most important words that people must understand if they to claim (or reclaim) their lives are **reality** and **choice**. The way we think the world works is what most of us call our **reality**. Essentially, reality is a set of societal agreements we either agree to or that we have been born into (though we must remember that we have choices in the way we interpret our reality.) We all have a set of stories that we have told ourselves about the way the world is or the way it works. These stories shape our identity, the roles we believe we should play in our families, amongst our friends, and even our understanding of who we are supposed to be in romantic relationships. Our stories are the way we interpret the world. I believe our story is our own individual worldview. Simply put, these stories are made up of the reality that we tell ourselves is true and the lessons the world has taught us about what is "real" or "not real" in the universe we live in. One tool that allows us a sense of freedom from the emotional bondage and the suffering caused by our fear of change or memories is an ability to ascribe *meaning* to them.

Art Opportunity:

For this art opportunity you have two choices: (you can either do one or both of these.)

First opportunity: Much like the opening breath prayer, draw a moment that you were grateful for recently. Include as much detail in the drawing as possible (for example, draw symbols or include descriptors for how it sounds, tastes, feels, etc.) Bask in that moment of gratitude—allow it to wash over you.

Second opportunity: Draw an experience that you previously viewed as negative or as a "stumbling block" in your life, but which you are now able to "reframe" into either a positive or productive part of your story. How does this event or situation now fit into the narrative of your life? How has it helped you and how can you build upon it in a positive way? Include as much detail in the drawing as possible.

> *Breathe in...you ARE ENOUGH*

> *Exhale...*

> *ENOUGH*

> *Inhale a sense of purpose*

> *Exhale...knowing you ARE ENOUGH*

MESSAGE TO YOUR INNER CHILD

4. *OUR INNER WOUNDED CHILD*

The way people respond to their momentary, minute to minute daily choices, what they might call their "life," is really an outline for how they are interpreting the world around them, a. It's a map of the stories we all tell ourselves about our place in the world. What holds most people back from achieving their goals is that the story map they have designed in their heads around what they are capable of doing or who they *think* they should or could be may not match their inner aspirations. As a child, when most of our story maps were designed, there were most likely several internal wounded-child stories that depicted a world of struggle and scarcity. The maps are full of stories that told you, "life is hard, opportunities are hard to come by,." These are childhood stories that may not have been *given space to evolve.* The intimate childhood stories that labeled you learning disabled, never enough or slow... the inner fat-kid stories when you were not picked for sports teams and always seemed to come in last... times when you felt picked on, bullied, or ridiculed for situations either beyond your control or just for being you... these inner childhood stories often have voices that made you feel like you would never, could never be enough. These inner wounded childhood stories are often made up of teacher voices, fragmented relatives, toxic friends, early boyfriends or girlfriends. They usually incorporate abuse stories, juvenile illnesses and disabilities. What they all have in common is they make people feel inwardly misunderstood, imperfect and never quite enough.

Psychologists call this internal dialogue and negative self-talk an "inner critic," believing we build these negative inner ideas from unconscious and conscious beliefs and biases, they. Such thoughts can easily interpret the way we process our capabilities and daily experiences. We can call this our *inner-wounded child voice*. Think back to your childhood. Did: did you see your coaches, teachers, school mates, family, church or even *society as a whole* as being *for* you or *against* you?

Some people say that the things we believe we are capable of are mapped out from choices we made early in our childhoods. In other words, our "worldview" is based upon choices most of us have forgotten the roots of. I am not saying that we see our role in the world based on childhood moments like the way were picked or not picked in Dodgeball. No, I am suggesting something a little deeper,... that our worldviews are based on *what you **thought** it meant about you*: when you were picked, who picked you and your interpretation of the people holding the game.

Richard Coolies' theory about how we build our self-image is called, "The Looking Glass Self." His argument is that we do not develop our image of ourselves based on what people *actually* think of us, but instead what we ***think*** they feel about us. How we interpret our place in the world then sets the stage for whether we see a world of abundance and opportunities or a dog-eat-dog world where there is only so much, and you had better fight for your small piece of it.

QUESTIONS TO CONSIDER:

Are there any childhood moments that you can recall which might have negatively affected your inner worldview and map?

Alternatively, are there any decisive positive childhood moments that you can recall-- (people, situations, or opportunities), which inspired or motivated you?

<u>**Art Opportunity:**</u>

Draw a picture of your older self giving advice to your younger self. What would you say to yourself as a child about what you've learned? What would you tell that young person to remember? What important lessons would you try to pass on? What would you tell them you are most grateful for, or not to take for granted? After you draw your older and younger selves, list as least three pieces of wisdom that you would like to pass along.

Slow your breath...
As you inhale watch your chest rise
As you exhale fully clear your lungs
Repeat
Fully breathing and being are acts of gratitude

WHAT IF I COULD BE STILL?

5. *WE ARE AFRAID TO BE STILL*

What would happen if you just let your mind stand still? No, not "treading water", but just sitting still-- without future desires or past regrets, just being mindfully still....

What are you afraid you might see or hear if you stood still? Do you think that your mind would ever stop racing with all of the to-dos, the "should have dones" or thoughts of all the people who would/could deem you weak for deciding to stand still?

What do you think would spook you first if you decided to stand still? Which thoughts do you think make the constant noise and movement necessary? Which ideas do you fear hearing the most? Is it the people you have felt a victim to, or the people you fear you have let down?

Do you think if you were in silence that you would be flooded with voices telling you you're "not enough"? Or are you more afraid that the silence would rupture an inner dam of views which, up to now, have been whispering, "You have so much more to offer. Why have you been hiding your gifts and talents?"

How do you fear all the different voices might present themselves? Would they sound like a disapproving or disappointed parent, friend, relative, boss, partner, or teacher? Are some of the influences you are distracted by not just from inside your own head? Are there actual relationships and/or situations which you fear you might have to deal with if you were to sit silent or stop moving for any length of time?

What would happen if you just let your mind stand still? No, not "treading water", but just sitting still?

Then again, maybe you do not want to stand still or risk a moment of silence because you fear the unknown. Do you fear the unknown thoughts that might come up if you do not maintain constant movement and noise to keep you distracted?

Instead of writing down or dwelling on what these piercing thoughts might sound like or the things you fear they would say, consider what you might say back to them if you had the time, energy or space. Would you respond to them with words of apology? Would you offer these voices an explanation for something? Or is there a sense of power you could use to express an opinion-- something you could say to reclaim your own voice or wrestle it back from them?

Art Opportunity:

Draw yourself in a place that you can safely and comfortably imagine yourself "being still." How are you feeling in this place? Are you able to be at ease? What would you need in this safe space in order to feel most able to relax? Draw as many details as you can image.

Plant your feet on the ground, as you take a
deep breath in...
Hold it... relax your shoulders
As you exhale ...smile
Inhale...the fullness of the day...hold it
Exhale...what is not
Inhale...what could be
Exhale...with your feet and life grounded in
now

LIES

6. THE GREAT LIE

T he great lie that most of us live with is this:

"Today must be like yesterday, and tomorrow is going to be like today."

There is a lot packed into this "great lie" ...within it there is our safety, our fears, and possibilities. Whether we think about it or not, most of us are comforted by the feeling that when we wake up in the morning, our home is there. It is also nice to see that our family, spouse, pets, job, car, friends, and food are still there when we wake up. Most of us go to sleep and wake up feeling reassured that what we left and who we were yesterday is going to follow us into the next day. One might say that this is one of the traps of successful people -- it can be easy for any of us to fall into the trap of believing that what we have said, made or shared in the world yesterday is going to speak for who we are going forward.

There is always going to be that one "thing" which we are either struggling to reach, or holding on to too tightly... perhaps it is a big business merger or sale, that one book or paper, that one presentation, that one sermon, that one idea, that one promotion or review, that one possession or title that we either have or want to acquire... and we think that those things are going to be the best of what we have to offer; they are what people are going to remember. This is a trap for two reasons: first, because when we define ourselves by our one significant achievement, it is easy to get complacent or indifferent and lean on the spoils of who we have been and what we have done. The second reason I call it a trap is that success is never stagnant; it shifts and changes just as all of life does. Just as the failures of our past do not define us, neither do the moments we have been successful.

For most of our lives, we are always in a constant motion of creating and recreating. Moments have life, death, and rebirth just as each breath we take has an inhale, hold, and an exhale before the next breath needs to give way. When there is no next breath, life ends. Think about it: if you choose not to take a new next breath, you are choosing not to live. Similarly, if you decide to hold a past breath and let that breath define you, you are choosing not to live much longer because you are trying to hold your breath. When we decide to stop creating and recreating in our relationships, work, art, friendships and ideas and instead hold on to what has already been, aren't we just trying to hold the breath we already took?

Deep down, I genuinely believe that the profusion of anxiety and depression in the U.S. today is wrapped up in this lie – today must be like yesterday, and tomorrow is going to be like today. In "Poke the Box" by Seth Godin, the author talks about the stumbling blocks that keep people from being productive in companies. A line that popped out to me is his personal definition of anxiety:

"I define anxiety as experiencing failure in advance . . . if you have anxiety about initiating a project, then, of course, you will associate risk with failure". (Seth Godin)

This definition strikes a chord for me because it seems to clearly describe so much of the anxiety that keeps people emotionally and creatively blocked. The most damaging part of the lie—that today must be like yesterday—is that people's suffering is borne out an attempt to hold today as it was yesterday, or as they believe or remember it was. The grief of a loss is natural; it means you truly loved and are going to miss the person or moment in time. But suffering is the act of trying to maintain that grief; it wants to fix things or hold them still and live for them as they once were.

Taking a moment to be mindfully grateful is a way you can honor yesterday, attempt to fully live your current day, and seek to rejoice in the abundance that could be tomorrow. Gratitude allows yesterday, today, and tomorrow to be their own parts of the full breadth of your life.

QUESTION TO CONSIDER:

What there one thing you are holding on to, that is causing you to suffer?

Art Opportunity:

Divide or fold your paper in half.
On one side write the word *"past"* at the top of the
page.

Beneath that word draw something, someone or
someplace that you feel you need to *"let go"* of...
something that may be holding you back.
Draw that thing, and then say a conscious prayer or
mindfully say a few words about **letting go and
releasing** that situation in order to make room for
the abundance of the present moment.

Next, on the other side of the paper, write the word
"present" at the top of the page.
This time, draw something, someone, or someplace
that you feel most grateful for **right now.** This may
be a particular person, place or thing that gives you
comfort and peace, helps you to breathe easier, helps
you to navigate the present moment, grounds you, or
puts you most at ease.

*Draw that thing, and then embrace the feeling of
gratitude and love that comes with it.*

Emptying the energy behind your eyes

There is stored up energy just behind your eyes, a welling of tear built up of fears, anxiety, and a collection of moments you are trying to hold as they were.

Find a quiet space and light a candle. A candle where you can watch the dancing of its flame.

Sit quietly with the flame, breathing fully. Inhale the heaviness of your fears, exhale hope, inhale anxiety and uncertainty, exhale peace and possibility. Repeat this with a full breath three times, still watching the dancing flame.

As the pocket of energy behind your eyes releases and your tears begin the fall, feel them fully on your cheek. Do not wipe them away, allow their sensation of freedom. Soften your shoulders, release your suffering, allow the tears to flow, feel fully the release, the freedom, the now.

*When the tears are through, blow out the candle. With
your energy emptied, close your eyes and, in a spirit of
gratitude, picture a person, place or moment you are
grateful for.*

*As you open your eyes and step away, consider how
you might express your appreciation for that person,
place or moment you pictured.
For it is not the thought, but the expression of
gratitude which ultimately frees you For it is not the
thought, but the expression of gratitude which
ultimately frees you.*

POWER

7. GRATITUDE SOUNDS WEAK

There has always been a debate in the world of

psychology over the concept of power. Is power a force that some people wield as a method of control and summation over other people? Or is power a give and take relationship where both parties have a role that they have agreed upon playing? The point is that power could simply be a construct of language.

A social scientist might point to Korzybski's maxim which states, "The map is not the territory." This theory points out that we should not ever be bound to any first interpretations of an event as being "real." Everything is simply an interpretation seen through the context, presuppositions, and choices which constitute our inner maps of the world. The power an event has over us has everything to do with the lens of our experience, worldview and how we understand our choices.

One example of this would be Dietrich Bonhoeffer, the great theologian and anti-Nazi dissident who famously said, "You can bring a Jew to their knees, but you can't make them worship you!" His point was that a Nazi soldier could force the Jew in a concentration camp to physically fall to their knees, but it was up to them to decide the meaning and level of power that the soldier had over their mind and spirit.

We decide what the moments in our lives mean. We give the challenges in our lives the level of power and control over what they mean to our future or our overall worldview. We decide what has power over us by our opinions, choices, and the meaning we ascribe to any given situation.

It is up to us to decide whether to interpret the loss of three jobs as a lesson in determining what we are best at, or what we no longer want to do ...or whether losing the third job means that we or the world has decided that we are worthless and unable of holding a job at all! Ultimately, we have the power to choose, and we are in control of the meaning we assign to the moments of our lives. Is something an obstacle or an opportunity?

Being grateful is another choice that involves power. A boss who is riding you at work or a fellow student who seems to be bullying you, can either empower or defeat you. In the light of gratitude, you can choose to see the world from the bully's eyes... what is their perspective? In the light of gratitude, you can choose to claim your worth and either report or challenge the bully. The power to prosecute or forgive is given to you within a spirit of gratitude.

Bonhoeffer's most famous texts was his April 1933 essay, "The Church and the Jewish Question."

QUESTION TO CONSIDER:

What power can we claim, and what authority do we need to take back, considering an abundant world of possibilities? What power can be opened because of our choice to be grateful?

Art opportunity:

Think of a situation (person, place or thing) that you believe has or had power over you. Draw what it would look like if the tables were turned and you had "power over" that thing/situation instead. Include as much detail as you feel able.

Big breath in...now exhale gratitude
Hold that moment
Inhale purpose... hold it
As you exhale... your shoulders drop, your body
relaxes
...hold that feeling
Inhale...a deep, deep sense of peace

NOT ENOUGH

8. FEEL OUT OF CONTROL

G ratitude reminds you of what you have, and

what you are capable of. However, it also tells you that
the world is not and never will be perfect. It will not
take you long before you are awakened to the profusion
of pain, loss, grief, and injustice in the world we live in.

Our mind asks, "how can we respond to a world filled
with struggle, pain, grief, and suffering with a spirit of
gratitude, knowing that we cannot fix it?" The list of
inadequacies goes on forever: Build a soup kitchen;
people will still be hungry. Open a shelter; people will

still be homeless. Recycle all your trash; there will still be landfills. Vote to raise or lower taxes...stand up for human rights and speak out against injustice; some people are still going to end up with more and some with less. Listen to your friends' depression and stand alongside your family with all of their anxieties and fears; you will never be able to remove all the grief in the world.

The same world, which is abundant with opportunities, is also plentiful in pain. Are we walking in a world which is never going to reach a perfect state of equality and peace? That question leads me to another question: a reader once wrote me and asked, "Is there such a thing as too much gratitude? How do you know when you have been grateful enough and can move on?"

My response to both questions is the same: there will always be a wealth of pain in the world, and you will never reach a place where you have shared enough gratitude.

Gratitude reminds us each day that the world is always moving, always shifting. Pain, suffering, and grief will never stay constant... but neither will joy, happiness, or peace. Because everything is continually growing, changing, shifting, creating, dying, and becoming anew, the world will never stop to reach a state of perfection. This is also why you cannot acquire enough "stuff" (money, power, success, etc.), because to say you have "enough" is to say that you are already whole and happy and will always stay that way. Pleasure, wholeness, and tranquility are in constant motion, just like discomfort, anguish, and grief; there can never be an equilibrium where any of them can be pinned down and remain as they are.

Gratitude is a path which you can choose to walk through the constant, ever-changing motion of life. Gratitude allows you to experience the abundance of life, not as a conclusion or answer, but as an ever-changing opportunity. You always have the choice to focus on what you do not have or what you do have. There are still two roads for you to choose to walk in light of an ever-changing world: one path interprets a world of ever-changing opportunities; the other road attempts to hold moments as they once were, in the belief that what *has been* is the best that life can ever be. You can look to your blessings, opportunities, and gifts, or you can focus on your obstacles and weaknesses, and experience the world and your life as broken.

Gratitude will not end people's suffering, pain, or the reality of grief once and for all. Instead, appreciation engages with and reinterprets the world, moment by moment -- from moments of grief to the remembrance of love. Indeed, gratitude takes us from trying to fix or return to an experience that ultimately leads to suffering, and puts us instead in a place that can focus on healing and allow for change, opportunities, and a life that can hold your past but is not defined by it.

Gratitude is the momentary choice to focus on abundance as a means of hope in this ever-changing world.

<u>Art Opportunity:</u>

1. Draw a "bridge of gratitude"—any representation of a bridge will do.

2. Then draw yourself somewhere on that bridge.

Think about these questions:

- Where are you on the bridge right now?
- What are you leaving behind?
- What are you walking towards? What are you grateful for along the way?

Draw as much detail as you feel able. Remember: it is not about the quality of the drawing... it is about the meaning and symbolism revealed behind it.

Take a deep breath and hold it....hold it...
hold it
Exhale.
No matter how long you hold a breath, life can only
continue if you exhale and open yourself to a new
breath.

SUFFERING & HEALING

9. NOSTALGIA

One-piece that shapes our worldview is rooted in

our understanding of how we weave the reality of

suffering and change. There is an old saying that says,

"the only thing in life guaranteed is death and taxes!" I

would like to amend that statement to say that the only

thing in life guaranteed is change (...and perhaps school

debt!)

There is an old Buddhist belief that suffering is born out

of a desire to keep things the way that you believe they

once were. Let's unpack this... what they are saying is
that people suffer most when they do not allow the
natural movement of life. They suffer when they try to
hold people, relationships, jobs, friendships, family,
their lifestyle, or their world in either a current or past
moment. And I said they suffer because they are trying
to hold things in a moment that they believe existed – it
may not actually have existed in the way they remember
it did, or at all, but -- it is a moment that they either
think they remember or desire to be so. I think a good
image for such suffering might be the feeling of treading
water, trying to stay in one place in a moving river.

This is not to say that the grief of a loss does not have its
place in life. Grief is a natural and inevitable response
to the loss or movement of something you have loved.
If you do not want to grieve, all you have to do is to
decide not to love or risk anything fully ...but then if you
have decided to never love or risk anything, have you
really ever lived? No, grief is natural; suffering is a
choice. Suffering is a choice to hold one's self in a state
of grief --to hold onto that moment of loss and not allow
the natural movement of new life to help us to shift,
grow and renew.

One of my favorite writers on the concept of mindful living is the Buddhist monk, Thich Ni Hon. In a message to his own students on his inevitable upcoming death, he said:

"Please do not build a stupa for me. Please do not put my ashes in a vase, lock me inside, and limit who I am. I know this will be difficult for some of you. If you must build a stupa, though, please make sure that you put a sign on it that says, 'I am not in here.' In addition, you can also put another sign that says, 'I am not out there either,' and a third sign that says, 'If I am anywhere, it is in your mindful breathing and in your peaceful steps.'"

The remedy to a moment of suffering is an internal choice to live fully in any given moment. A life of gratitude is about choosing to engage in life's changes. It is choice each day, each moment, each step, each breath to connect rather than disconnect. Meditation and prayer are not meant to be moments of disconnect or a time to hold things as they are. Prayer and meditation are about deciding to be fully present, fully alive, and completely engaged, even if only for a moment.

Suffering often occurs in isolation, much like depression. As we suffer, we make a choice to stand alone and to push people away. We may say to ourselves, "How could they ever understand?" Healing, in contrast, occurs in community ...not a random community, but a trusted, close, emotionally, or spiritually intimate community. Sometimes the community is three, sometimes two, and it can even be just one close friend who is willing to hold our story, walk with us on our journey, and be fully present with us. These sacred connections are not about fixing or changing anything. They are a community willing to embrace, stand with, or hold up the sufferer. They are voices that simply say, "You are not alone."

The door to connection and the building of such a community is born out of a spirit of gratitude. Healing is a daily choice to seek and connect with those people and moments which are for you rather than against you.

Fixing, much like suffering, is usually about trying to make a moment something it was. Fixing is about returning someone or something back to a simpler or perfect state. We need to remember that even if a bone heals when it is bandaged, it is not the same bone; it is a new creation. Just as no two snowflakes are the same, likewise, there is no new relationship that will be like the last. There is also no amount of suffering that can change the fact that life is in a constant state of change and movement. If we can seek to heal rather than fix our lives, we are allowing the possibility of new life, new creations, and new possibilities.

Art Opportunity:

Divide your paper into two sides (just draw a line in the middle).

On one side of the paper draw an area of your life that you would like to "fix". This may be a particular situation that you are trying to hold as it is, as it was, or as you desired it to be... something that isn't "perfect".

Next, on the other side of the paper draw what it might look like if you let that particular situation to "flow into the river of change"... if you let it go, and allowed it to change into whatever it is meant to become. This may either mean accepting it completely as it is or releasing it and allowing it to grow and find its full potential. What does it look like when you let it go? How does the situation change when you stop trying to control the things that you ultimately cannot control, and focus instead on the things that are within your power to change or accept?

WORKBOOK

CLAIMING THE DAY

<u>CLAIM YOUR DAY: WORKBOOK</u>

A book on gratitude is difficult to write because so much of the power and transformation of its study comes out of the inner exploration of one's own experiences, shared stories and worldview. I as a writer can share what my obstacles or obstructions are to gratitude, but only by a reader diving in and exploring their own questions and experiences is any lasting change in perspective possible. It is almost impossible for someone to explain how a life of gratitude will change their worldview with words. There is a Buddhist Dharma teaching where monks would actually smack their students on the head with a stick as a way to tangibly teach them how to be mindfully and be in the – now. The following is a workbook is meant to be this type of object lesson –without the pain of getting your head hit! The workbook allows you to exhale your thoughts in a tangible and meaningful way. The tool made up of quotes and questions is meant to offer inner and outer exploration in a tangible and yet personal way. The workbook will allow you to reflect in a mindful way, not just on your daily expenses, but on a life lived with a full breath of gratitude.

The **Claim Your Day workbook** is made up of two exercises. The first page offers a quote and a reflective question for you to dive into. The second page holds the Daily Five & One questions. You are welcome to answer the questions either in a second notebook or simply jot down a one or two line note within the clipboard. The power of the Daily Five & One is not in how much you chose to write. These questions when answered daily will begin to restructure the way you look at conversations, opportunities and your overall day.

DAILY FIVE & ONE

Honestly, I wanted to share the five questions I try to start each day with. They move my morning mind from a space of scarcity to one of abundance. Considering these questions reminds me that the world (or God) is constantly opening for me, rather than closing in around me. However, as I recalled my five questions, I realized there are actually SIX! So, I have decided to name this exercise **My Daily Five & One**, because I think each of these six questions in some way shape the way I see my day in a special way.

1. **I was so grateful yesterday that I got to:**

2. **I was inspired yesterday when:**

3. **It really helped me yesterday when:**

4. **I had a moment of peace yesterday when:**

5. **Yesterday I was so glad I ran into:**

1. **I had to smile yesterday when:**

(But you only have to do five questions if you want!)

With time, the exercise moves your mind from the moment worries of need to those of abundance. When the questions are done daily, your mind will begin to teach itself to look for moments during your day that you will be able to use in answering the questions the next day. Suddenly your mind will begin to notice moments of opportunity rather than needs throughout your day.

The quotes and questions are meant to redirect your inner perspective. It is the daily consideration of the Daily Five & One which has the most potential for reshaping not just your day, but your working inner story and ultimately your working worldview.

CLAIMING THE DAY

Date: _____ *Day:* _____ *Time:* _____

> "A man's indebtedness is not virtue;
> his repayment is. Virtue begins when he
> dedicates himself actively to the job
> of gratitude." — Ruth Benedict

What attributes do you find virtuous in a person?

DAILY FIVE & ONE

1. I was so grateful yesterday that I got to:

2. I was inspired yesterday when:

3. It really helped me yesterday when:

4. I had a moment of peace yesterday when:

5. Yesterday I was so glad I ran into:

1. I had to smile yesterday when:

CLAIMING THE DAY

Date: _____ *Day:* _____ *Time:* _____

"Ambition breaks the ties of blood, and forgets the obligations of gratitude."
- Sallust

In your daily push to be successful, what/who do you most often forget to be grateful for?

DAILY FIVE & ONE

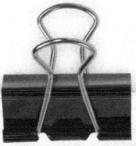

1. I was so grateful yesterday that I got to:

2. I was inspired yesterday when:

3. It really helped me yesterday when:

4. I had a moment of peace yesterday when:

5. Yesterday I was so glad I ran into:

1. I had to smile yesterday when:

CLAIMING THE DAY

Date: _____ *Day:* _____ *Time:* _____

"Appreciation can make a day, even change a life. Your willingness to put it into words is all that is necessary." — Margaret Cousins

Make a list of the people that make your life the most difficult. Then, once you have finished, name one time they acted outside their norm and did something that benefited you.

DAILY FIVE & ONE

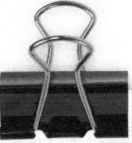

1. I was so grateful yesterday that I got to:

2. I was inspired yesterday when:

3. It really helped me yesterday when:

4. I had a moment of peace yesterday when:

5. Yesterday I was so glad I ran into:

1. I had to smile yesterday when:

CLAIMING THE DAY

Date: _____ *Day:* _____ *Time:* _____

"As we express our gratitude, we must
never forget that the highest
appreciation is not to utter words, but
to live by them." — John F. Kennedy

**From today's list of appreciation, pick one item
and write about a way you could show your
gratitude for it during the day tomorrow.**

DAILY FIVE & ONE

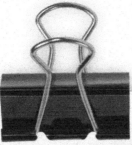

1. I was so grateful yesterday that I got to:

2. I was inspired yesterday when:

3. It really helped me yesterday when:

4. I had a moment of peace yesterday when:

5. Yesterday I was so glad I ran into:

1. I had to smile yesterday when:

CLAIMING THE DAY

Date: _____ *Day:* _____ *Time:* _____

> "Develop an attitude of gratitude, and give thanks for everything that happens to you, knowing that every step forward is a step toward achieving something bigger and better than your current situation." — Brian Tracy

From all your current life goals right now, what is one thing that has happened in the last week that was a step forward toward that goal?

DAILY FIVE & ONE

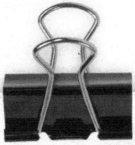

1. I was so grateful yesterday that I got to:

2. I was inspired yesterday when:

3. It really helped me yesterday when:

4. I had a moment of peace yesterday when:

5. Yesterday I was so glad I ran into:

1. I had to smile yesterday when:

CLAIMING THE DAY

Date: _____ *Day:* _____ *Time:* _____

> "Don't pray when it rains if you don't
> pray when the sun shines." — Satchell
> Paige

**It is easy to think about all the things that you
have not been able to accomplish. Write a short
paragraph describing what aspects of your life
are working right now.**

DAILY FIVE & ONE

1. I was so grateful yesterday that I got to:

2. I was inspired yesterday when:

3. It really helped me yesterday when:

4. I had a moment of peace yesterday when:

5. Yesterday I was so glad I ran into:

1. I had to smile yesterday when:

CLAIMING THE DAY

Date: _____ *Day:* _____ *Time:* _____

> "Every professional athlete owes a debt
> of gratitude to the fans and
> management, and pays an installment
> every time he plays. He should never
> miss a payment." — Bobby Hull

Make a list of the people in your life who have always been your cheerleaders.

DAILY FIVE & ONE

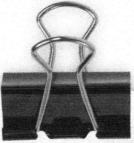

1. I was so grateful yesterday that I got to:

2. I was inspired yesterday when:

3. It really helped me yesterday when:

4. I had a moment of peace yesterday when:

5. Yesterday I was so glad I ran into:

1. I had to smile yesterday when:

CLAIMING THE DAY

Date: _____ *Day:* _____ *Time:* _____

> "Gratefulness is the key to a happy life that we hold in our hands, because if we are not grateful, then no matter how much we have we will not be happy — because we will always want to have something else or something more." — David Steindl-Rast

Is there a friend from your past who you should say thank you to?

DAILY FIVE & ONE

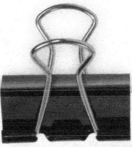

1. I was so grateful yesterday that I got to:

2. I was inspired yesterday when:

3. It really helped me yesterday when:

4. I had a moment of peace yesterday when:

5. Yesterday I was so glad I ran into:

1. I had to smile yesterday when:

CLAIMING THE DAY

Date: _____ *Day:* _____ *Time:* _____

> "Gratitude bestows reverence, allowing us to encounter everyday epiphanies, those transcendent moments of awe that change forever how we experience life and the world." — John Milton

What things have you said you needed before you thought you could be happy? Are there things today that you think you need to feel fulfilled? Write about what you believe those missing things would bring you if you had them.

DAILY FIVE & ONE

1. I was so grateful yesterday that I got to:

2. I was inspired yesterday when:

3. It really helped me yesterday when:

4. I had a moment of peace yesterday when:

5. Yesterday I was so glad I ran into:

1. I had to smile yesterday when:

CLAIMING THE DAY

Date: _____ *Day:* _____ *Time:* _____

> "Gratitude changes the pangs of memory
> into a tranquil joy." — Dietrich
> Bonhoeffer

Are there any challenges that seem to have faded since you began completing your daily gratitude list?

DAILY FIVE & ONE

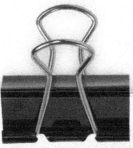

1. I was so grateful yesterday that I got to:

2. I was inspired yesterday when:

3. It really helped me yesterday when:

4. I had a moment of peace yesterday when:

5. Yesterday I was so glad I ran into:

1. I had to smile yesterday when:

CLAIMING THE DAY

Date: _____ *Day:* _____ *Time:* _____

> "Gratitude helps you to grow and
> expand; gratitude brings joy and
> laughter into your life and into the
> lives of all those around you." –
> Eileen Caddy

Has your expression of gratitude affected anyone's life around you in a noticeable way?

DAILY FIVE & ONE

1. I was so grateful yesterday that I got to:

2. I was inspired yesterday when:

3. It really helped me yesterday when:

4. I had a moment of peace yesterday when:

5. Yesterday I was so glad I ran into:

1. I had to smile yesterday when:

CLAIMING THE DAY

Date: _____ *Day:* _____ *Time:* _____

"Gratitude is a burden upon our
imperfect nature, and we are but too
willing to ease ourselves of it, or at
least to lighten it as much as we can."
— Philip Stanhope

**Sometimes it is easier for us to find
circumstances or people to blame for our
struggles. Can you think of situations or people
you have blamed instead of taking
responsibility for your own actions?**

DAILY FIVE & ONE

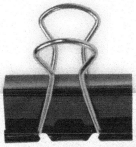

1. I was so grateful yesterday that I got to:

2. I was inspired yesterday when:

3. It really helped me yesterday when:

4. I had a moment of peace yesterday when:

5. Yesterday I was so glad I ran into:

1. I had to smile yesterday when:

CLAIMING THE DAY

Date: _____ *Day:* _____ *Time:* _____

> "Gratitude is a duty which ought to be paid, but which none have a right to expect." — Jean-Jacques Rousseau

Do you think the above statement is true? Are you ever one of those people who expect to be thanked for the things you do?

DAILY FIVE & ONE

1. I was so grateful yesterday that I got to:

2. I was inspired yesterday when:

3. It really helped me yesterday when:

4. I had a moment of peace yesterday when:

5. Yesterday I was so glad I ran into:

1. I had to smile yesterday when:

CLAIMING THE DAY

Date: _____ *Day:* _____ *Time:* _____

"Gratitude is one of those things that cannot be bought. It must be born with men, or else all the obligations in the world will not create it." — Edward F. Halifax

Have you ever experienced fake praise? How could you tell it was not sincere gratitude? How can people tell if the compliments you give them are sincere?

DAILY FIVE & ONE

1. I was so grateful yesterday that I got to:

2. I was inspired yesterday when:

3. It really helped me yesterday when:

4. I had a moment of peace yesterday when:

5. Yesterday I was so glad I ran into:

1. I had to smile yesterday when:

CLAIMING THE DAY

Date: _____ *Day:* _____ *Time:* _____

> "Gratitude is the fairest blossom which springs from the soul." — Henry Ward Beecher

When you receive a sincere compliment from someone, how does it change your relationship with them?

DAILY FIVE & ONE

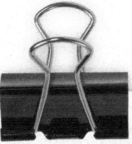

1. I was so grateful yesterday that I got to:

2. I was inspired yesterday when:

3. It really helped me yesterday when:

4. I had a moment of peace yesterday when:

5. Yesterday I was so glad I ran into:

1. I had to smile yesterday when:

CLAIMING THE DAY

Date: _____ *Day:* _____ *Time:* _____

> "Gratitude is the inward feeling of kindness received. Thankfulness is the natural impulse to express that feeling. Thanksgiving is the following of that impulse." — Henry Van Dyke

What has kept you from expressing thanksgiving in the past? What keeps you from expressing thankfulness today?

DAILY FIVE & ONE

1. I was so grateful yesterday that I got to:

2. I was inspired yesterday when:

3. It really helped me yesterday when:

4. I had a moment of peace yesterday when:

5. Yesterday I was so glad I ran into:

1. I had to smile yesterday when:

CLAIMING THE DAY

Date: _____ *Day:* _____ *Time:* _____

"Gratitude is the sign of noble souls."
- Aesop

How would you describe a "noble soul"?

DAILY FIVE & ONE

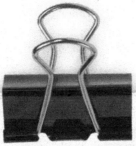

1. I was so grateful yesterday that I got to:

2. I was inspired yesterday when:

3. It really helped me yesterday when:

4. I had a moment of peace yesterday when:

5. Yesterday I was so glad I ran into:

1. I had to smile yesterday when:

CLAIMING THE DAY

Date: _____ *Day:* _____ *Time:* _____

"Gratitude is the most exquisite form
of courtesy." — Jacques Maritain

**What do you think keeps some people from
truly appreciating you? How could you live
your life today in a way is worthy of respect --by
at least yourself?**

DAILY FIVE & ONE

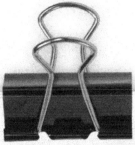

1. I was so grateful yesterday that I got to:

2. I was inspired yesterday when:

3. It really helped me yesterday when:

4. I had a moment of peace yesterday when:

5. Yesterday I was so glad I ran into:

1. I had to smile yesterday when:

CLAIMING THE DAY

Date: _____ *Day:* _____ *Time:* _____

> "Gratitude is when memory is stored in
> the heart and not in the mind." —
> Lionel Hampton

If you could lay down your past mistakes and fears of failing in the future, what would you do today?

DAILY FIVE & ONE

1. I was so grateful yesterday that I got to:

2. I was inspired yesterday when:

3. It really helped me yesterday when:

4. I had a moment of peace yesterday when:

5. Yesterday I was so glad I ran into:

1. I had to smile yesterday when:

CLAIMING THE DAY

Date: _____ *Day:* _____ *Time:* _____

"Gratitude isn't a burdening emotion."
— Loretta Young

We always think of all the things we need before we could truly be happy. What would you be happy about if you did not need those things?

DAILY FIVE & ONE

1. I was so grateful yesterday that I got to:

2. I was inspired yesterday when:

3. It really helped me yesterday when:

4. I had a moment of peace yesterday when:

5. Yesterday I was so glad I ran into:

1. I had to smile yesterday when:

CLAIMING THE DAY

Date: _____ *Day:* _____ *Time:* _____

> "Gratitude makes sense of our past,
> brings peace for today, and creates a
> vision for tomorrow." — Melody Beattie

If yesterday did not dictate who you had to be today, what would you free yourself to create, do or say today?

DAILY FIVE & ONE

1. I was so grateful yesterday that I got to:

2. I was inspired yesterday when:

3. It really helped me yesterday when:

4. I had a moment of peace yesterday when:

5. Yesterday I was so glad I ran into:

1. I had to smile yesterday when:

CLAIMING THE DAY

Date: _____ *Day:* _____ *Time:* _____

> "Gratitude to gratitude always gives
> birth." - Sophocles

Is there anyone in your life that you feel is truly grateful for you? How do they show it? How can you tell they are grateful for you? How might you return that gratitude to them in a tangible way?

DAILY FIVE & ONE

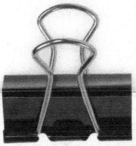

1. I was so grateful yesterday that I got to:

2. I was inspired yesterday when:

3. It really helped me yesterday when:

4. I had a moment of peace yesterday when:

5. Yesterday I was so glad I ran into:

1. I had to smile yesterday when:

CLAIMING THE DAY

Date: _____ *Day:* _____ *Time:* _____

"Gratitude unlocks the fullness of
life. It turns what we have into
enough, and more. It turns denial into
acceptance, chaos to order, confusion
to clarity. It can turn a meal into a
feast, a house into a home, a stranger
into a friend." — Melody Beattie

**Since you began utilizing this gratitude journal,
how has your life changed? Is there any way
you see people around you differently?**

DAILY FIVE & ONE

1. I was so grateful yesterday that I got to:

2. I was inspired yesterday when:

3. It really helped me yesterday when:

4. I had a moment of peace yesterday when:

5. Yesterday I was so glad I ran into:

1. I had to smile yesterday when:

CLAIMING THE DAY

Date: _____ *Day:* _____ *Time:* _____

"Happiness cannot be traveled to, owned, earned, worn or consumed. Happiness is the spiritual experience of living every minute with love, grace, and gratitude." — Denis Waitley "Act with kindness, but do not expect gratitude." - Proverb

How would you define happiness for yourself?

DAILY FIVE & ONE

1. I was so grateful yesterday that I got to:

2. I was inspired yesterday when:

3. It really helped me yesterday when:

4. I had a moment of peace yesterday when:

5. Yesterday I was so glad I ran into:

1. I had to smile yesterday when:

CLAIMING THE DAY

Date: _____ *Day:* _____ *Time:* _____

"Happiness is itself a kind of gratitude." — Joseph Wood Krutch

What would the picture of a happy world look like? It be small or big, but how might you paint a stroke in that picture of a happy world today?

DAILY FIVE & ONE

1. I was so grateful yesterday that I got to:

2. I was inspired yesterday when:

3. It really helped me yesterday when:

4. I had a moment of peace yesterday when:

5. Yesterday I was so glad I ran into:

1. I had to smile yesterday when:

CLAIMING THE DAY

Date: _____ *Day:* _____ *Time:* _____

> "If the only prayer you said in your
> whole life was, 'thank you,' that would
> suffice." — Meister Eckhart

What have you forgotten so say thank you to God for lately?

DAILY FIVE & ONE

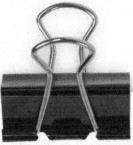

1. I was so grateful yesterday that I got to:

2. I was inspired yesterday when:

3. It really helped me yesterday when:

4. I had a moment of peace yesterday when:

5. Yesterday I was so glad I ran into:

1. I had to smile yesterday when:

CLAIMING THE DAY

Date: _____ *Day:* _____ *Time:* _____

> "It's a sign of mediocrity when you demonstrate gratitude with moderation."
> — Roberto Benigni

Was there ever a time in your life when you were just gratful that you were able to take the next breath?

DAILY FIVE & ONE

1. I was so grateful yesterday that I got to:

2. I was inspired yesterday when:

3. It really helped me yesterday when:

4. I had a moment of peace yesterday when:

5. Yesterday I was so glad I ran into:

1. I had to smile yesterday when:

CLAIMING THE DAY

Date: _____ Day: _____ Time: _____

"Joy is a heart full and a mind
purified by gratitude." — Marietta
McCarty

**If you could describe a difference between joy
and happiness, what would that difference be?**

DAILY FIVE & ONE

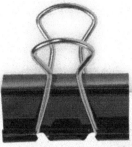

1. I was so grateful yesterday that I got to:

2. I was inspired yesterday when:

3. It really helped me yesterday when:

4. I had a moment of peace yesterday when:

5. Yesterday I was so glad I ran into:

1. I had to smile yesterday when:

CLAIMING THE DAY

Date: _____ *Day:* _____ *Time:* _____

"Joy is the simplest form of
gratitude." — Karl Barth

When life seems difficult, what represents a moment of joy?

DAILY FIVE & ONE

1. I was so grateful yesterday that I got to:

2. I was inspired yesterday when:

3. It really helped me yesterday when:

4. I had a moment of peace yesterday when:

5. Yesterday I was so glad I ran into:

1. I had to smile yesterday when:

CLAIMING THE DAY

Date: _____ *Day:* _____ *Time:* _____

> "Kindness trumps greed: it asks for sharing. Kindness trumps fear: it calls forth gratefulness and love. Kindness trumps even stupidity, for with sharing and love, one learns." — Marc Estrin

Thinking back to yesterday, was there a moment of kindness that someone showed you that you did not expect? Describe the interaction.

DAILY FIVE & ONE

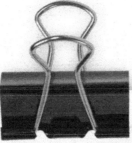

1. I was so grateful yesterday that I got to:

2. I was inspired yesterday when:

3. It really helped me yesterday when:

4. I had a moment of peace yesterday when:

5. Yesterday I was so glad I ran into:

1. I had to smile yesterday when:

CLAIMING THE DAY

Date: _____ *Day:* _____ *Time:* _____

"Let us be grateful to people who make us happy; they are the charming gardeners who make our souls blossom."
— Marcel Proust

Who is most difficult for you to be grateful for? Can you list three things that you are grateful for them for doing for you?

DAILY FIVE & ONE

1. I was so grateful yesterday that I got to:

2. I was inspired yesterday when:

3. It really helped me yesterday when:

4. I had a moment of peace yesterday when:

5. Yesterday I was so glad I ran into:

1. I had to smile yesterday when:

CLAIMING THE DAY

Date: _____ *Day:* _____ *Time:* _____

> "Maybe the only thing worse than having to give gratitude constantly is having to accept it." -William Faulkner

What makes you nervous about people who show too much gratitude to you? Is it that you do not think that they are sincere? Do you think you don't deserve their gratitude? Do you you fear they will eventually see through to the way you see yourself?

DAILY FIVE & ONE

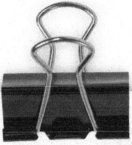

1. I was so grateful yesterday that I got to:

2. I was inspired yesterday when:

3. It really helped me yesterday when:

4. I had a moment of peace yesterday when:

5. Yesterday I was so glad I ran into:

1. I had to smile yesterday when:

CLAIMING THE DAY

Date: _____ *Day:* _____ *Time:* _____

"Next to ingratitude the most painful
thing to bear is gratitude." — Henry
Ward Beecher

**With all your imperfections, what is something
you are grateful for about yourself today? Why
was this exercise difficult for you? Is it okay for
you to be grateful for who you are?**

DAILY FIVE & ONE

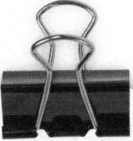

1. I was so grateful yesterday that I got to:

2. I was inspired yesterday when:

3. It really helped me yesterday when:

4. I had a moment of peace yesterday when:

5. Yesterday I was so glad I ran into:

1. I had to smile yesterday when:

CLAIMING THE DAY

Date: _____ *Day:* _____ *Time:* _____

> "No one who achieves success does so
> without acknowledging the help of
> others. The wise and confident
> acknowledge this help with gratitude."
> — Alfred North Whitehead

Do you remember a person in your life that really taught you how to give thanks? What words did they use? How did they act? Why did you or did you not believe them?

DAILY FIVE & ONE

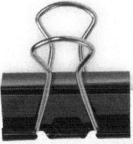

1. I was so grateful yesterday that I got to:

2. I was inspired yesterday when:

3. It really helped me yesterday when:

4. I had a moment of peace yesterday when:

5. Yesterday I was so glad I ran into:

1. I had to smile yesterday when:

CLAIMING THE DAY

Date: _____ *Day:* _____ *Time:* _____

> "One can never pay in gratitude: one
> can only pay 'in kind' somewhere else
> in life." — Anne Morrow Lindbergh

The problem with reciprocity, doing something to get something, is that it is most often fake. How are people able to tell if your gratitude for them is sincere?

DAILY FIVE & ONE

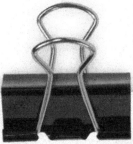

1. I was so grateful yesterday that I got to:

2. I was inspired yesterday when:

3. It really helped me yesterday when:

4. I had a moment of peace yesterday when:

5. Yesterday I was so glad I ran into:

1. I had to smile yesterday when:

CLAIMING THE DAY

Date: _____ *Day:* _____ *Time:* _____

> "One looks back with appreciation to
> the brilliant teachers, but with
> gratitude to those who touched our
> human feelings. The curriculum is so
> much necessary raw material, but warmth
> is the vital element for the growing
> plant and for the soul of the child."
> - Carl Jung

If you describe to a child what gratitude looked like, what colors, sounds or images would you use?

DAILY FIVE & ONE

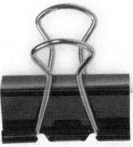

1. I was so grateful yesterday that I got to:

2. I was inspired yesterday when:

3. It really helped me yesterday when:

4. I had a moment of peace yesterday when:

5. Yesterday I was so glad I ran into:

1. I had to smile yesterday when:

CLAIMING THE DAY

Date: _____ *Day:* _____ *Time:* _____

> "One of the surest evidences of
> friendship that one individual can
> display to another is telling him
> gently of a fault. If any other can
> excel it, it is listening to such a
> disclosure with gratitude, and amending
> the error." — Edward G. Bulwer-Lytton

Is there someone in your life that you do not mind taking criticism from? What did they do to earn that level of trust? Next, look deep in your spirit and ask yourself, are you someone that someone special could trust to offer them criticism?

DAILY FIVE & ONE

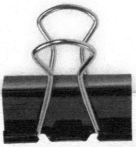

1. I was so grateful yesterday that I got to:

2. I was inspired yesterday when:

3. It really helped me yesterday when:

4. I had a moment of peace yesterday when:

5. Yesterday I was so glad I ran into:

1. I had to smile yesterday when:

CLAIMING THE DAY

Date: _____ *Day:* _____ *Time:* _____

> "Thankfulness is the beginning of
> gratitude. Gratitude is the completion
> of thankfulness. Thankfulness may
> consist merely of words. Gratitude is
> shown in acts." — Henri Frederic Amiel

Think about your interactions yesterday. By your actions alone, would the people around you have known how grateful you are for them? Why do you think they knew or did not know how grateful you were for them?

DAILY FIVE & ONE

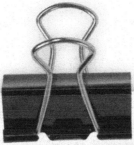

1. I was so grateful yesterday that I got to:

2. I was inspired yesterday when:

3. It really helped me yesterday when:

4. I had a moment of peace yesterday when:

5. Yesterday I was so glad I ran into:

1. I had to smile yesterday when:

CLAIMING THE DAY

Date: _____ *Day:* _____ *Time:* _____

> "The debt of gratitude we owe our mother and father goes forward, not backward. What we owe our parents is the bill presented to us by our children." — Nancy Friday

Is there a way you show your children or friends your level of gratitude for them that mimics the way your parents show you how much they appreciate you?

DAILY FIVE & ONE

1. I was so grateful yesterday that I got to:

2. I was inspired yesterday when:

3. It really helped me yesterday when:

4. I had a moment of peace yesterday when:

5. Yesterday I was so glad I ran into:

1. I had to smile yesterday when:

CLAIMING THE DAY

Date: _____ Day: _____ Time: _____

> "The deepest craving of human nature is the need to be appreciated." — William James

Without naming your parents or grandparents, who is someone from your childhood you are grateful for? How did you know them, and what did they do or say that inspired you?

DAILY FIVE & ONE

1. I was so grateful yesterday that I got to:

2. I was inspired yesterday when:

3. It really helped me yesterday when:

4. I had a moment of peace yesterday when:

5. Yesterday I was so glad I ran into:

1. I had to smile yesterday when:

CLAIMING THE DAY

Date: _____ *Day:* _____ *Time:* _____

> "The essence of all beautiful art, all
> great art, is gratitude." — Friedrich
> Nietzsche

If you could depict gratitude as a piece of art, what would its attributes be? Can you recall a piece of art that you think best depicts gratitude? (If not, take a moment in Google images to research a piece of art that you think depicts your own image.)

DAILY FIVE & ONE

1. I was so grateful yesterday that I got to:

2. I was inspired yesterday when:

3. It really helped me yesterday when:

4. I had a moment of peace yesterday when:

5. Yesterday I was so glad I ran into:

1. I had to smile yesterday when:

CLAIMING THE DAY

Date: _____ *Day:* _____ *Time:* _____

> "The hardest arithmetic to master is that which enables us to count our blessings." — Eric Hoffer

Think back on your whole day yesterday. Now take a moment to count the number of times that you felt blessed by God.

DAILY FIVE & ONE

1. I was so grateful yesterday that I got to:

2. I was inspired yesterday when:

3. It really helped me yesterday when:

4. I had a moment of peace yesterday when:

5. Yesterday I was so glad I ran into:

1. I had to smile yesterday when:

CLAIMING THE DAY

Date: _____ *Day:* _____ *Time:* _____

> "There is as much greatness of mind in
> acknowledging a good turn, as in doing
> it." - Seneca

Is there any hard situation going on in your life right now that you could reframe in a spirit of gratitude?

DAILY FIVE & ONE

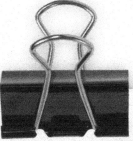

1. I was so grateful yesterday that I got to:

2. I was inspired yesterday when:

3. It really helped me yesterday when:

4. I had a moment of peace yesterday when:

5. Yesterday I was so glad I ran into:

1. I had to smile yesterday when:

CLAIMING THE DAY

Date: _____ *Day:* _____ *Time:* _____

> "To educate yourself for the feeling of gratitude means to take nothing for granted, but to always seek out and value the kind that will stand behind the action. Nothing that is done for you is a matter of course. Everything originates in a will for the good, which is directed at you. – Albert Schweitzer

If you were to try to train yourself to be more grateful during your day tomorrow, what would be the most difficult part?

DAILY FIVE & ONE

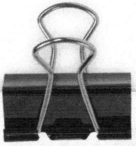

1. I was so grateful yesterday that I got to:

2. I was inspired yesterday when:

3. It really helped me yesterday when:

4. I had a moment of peace yesterday when:

5. Yesterday I was so glad I ran into:

1. I had to smile yesterday when:

CLAIMING THE DAY

Date: _____ *Day:* _____ *Time:* _____

> "We are told that people stay in love because of chemistry, or because they remain intrigued with each other, because of many kindnesses, because of luck. But part of it has got to be forgiveness and gratefulness." — Ellen Goodman

It may be easy to list the ways you are grateful for someone you love; but if you had a list of the ways that make it hard to be grateful for someone you love, what would be the hardest one be?

DAILY FIVE & ONE

1. I was so grateful yesterday that I got to:

2. I was inspired yesterday when:

3. It really helped me yesterday when:

4. I had a moment of peace yesterday when:

5. Yesterday I was so glad I ran into:

1. I had to smile yesterday when:

CLAIMING THE DAY

Date: _____ *Day:* _____ *Time:* _____

"When you are grateful fear disappears and abundance appears." — Tony Robbins

What is the most difficut thing in your life to be grateful for?

DAILY FIVE & ONE

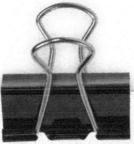

1. I was so grateful yesterday that I got to:

2. I was inspired yesterday when:

3. It really helped me yesterday when:

4. I had a moment of peace yesterday when:

5. Yesterday I was so glad I ran into:

1. I had to smile yesterday when:

CLAIMING THE DAY

Date: _____ *Day:* _____ *Time:* _____

> "You say grace before meals. All right.
> But I say grace before the concert and
> the opera, and grace before the play
> and pantomime, and grace before I open
> a book, and grace before sketching,
> painting, swimming, fencing, boxing,
> walking, playing, dancing…

If you could write a song lyric or poem that best depicted how grateful you were for someone or something special happening in your life right now, how would it sound?

DAILY FIVE & ONE

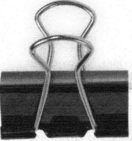

1. I was so grateful yesterday that I got to:

2. I was inspired yesterday when:

3. It really helped me yesterday when:

4. I had a moment of peace yesterday when:

5. Yesterday I was so glad I ran into:

1. I had to smile yesterday when:

Continue the conversation.

Facebook group: Full Breath of Gratitude, to share stories and participate in discussions around gratitude and abundant living.

Subscribe to channels: FullBreathofGratitude: Tiktok, Youtube, Facebook

For other gratitude workbooks and information on future journals, books and projects visit: fullbreathofgratitude.com

To book speaking, workshop or consulting services for individual, Church, business or nonprofits please contact: Chris Craig Stolenhoursconsulting@gmail.com 70P-urp-ose9, (707-877-6739), Website: FullBreathofGratitude.com